I0412441

Rush Limbaugh Was Right

Liberals who saw the light thanks to Rush Limbaugh

Edited by Peter Cornswalled

Contact Peter Cornswalled
Peter.Cornswalled@gmail.com

"Never be afraid to raise your voice for honesty and truth and compassion against injustice and lying and greed. If people all over the world...would do this, it would change the earth."
— William Faulkner

Introduction

During his long and successful broadcasting career, Rush Limbaugh has become the role model for all conservative talk show hosts. His acolytes permeate the radio world, reaching into podcasting and a wide range of "New Media" outlets. While the liberal, Main Stream Media (MSM) slanders him with insults and abuse, he stands fast with a reputation for honesty, integrity and accuracy unparalleled in the news industry.

Even some of Rush's long time fans may not realize that Rush has a history of showing liberals the light. He doesn't just help his self-proclaimed "Dittoheads" stand firm against the onslaught of a degenerate media and corrupt government, he helps liberals, moderates and lapsed conservatives alike see their way back to reason, rationality and sanity. This book tells the stories of times the scales fell from a person's eyes because of the education provided by Rush Limbaugh. Who could expect less from a man with "talent on loan from God?"

Hillary's Shoes

Edward from Florida.

The news that someone had chucked a shoe at Hillary Clinton was odd to hear. I remembered the footage of George W. Bush being on the receiving end of the same treatment in the Middle East. There it had been not just an assault but an attempt at an insult. In a land covered with sand and camel dung, the soles of your shoes are supposed to be the single most insulting thing you can show somebody. Just like Americans used to throw rotting vegetables at politicians they hated, people in the Middle East throw old shoes.

Why'd someone throw a shoe at Hillary?

I looked high and low, but I never found a suitable answer in the Mainstream Media. My favorite news sources all failed me. CNN had more than one version of events, MSNBC was muddled and confused. I posted to Twitter asking if any of my friends knew any good sources of information and one of them, as a joke, posted a link to Rush Limbaugh's coverage of the incident.

http://www.rushlimbaugh.com/daily/2014/04/14/quick_hits_page

I started reading, expecting to be infuriated as usual.

> *Is the media looping this and showing it over and over again like they did when Bush got targeted with those shoes? (interruption) They're not? Well, I wonder why? I wonder why. Seriously, this is a very offensive thing. I don't care what culture you are, when somebody throws a shoe at you, it's an insult. If Hillary looked really suave and debonair in missing the shoe -- if she had a really, really fast, brilliant comeback -- why wouldn't they be looping this and showing it over and over again?*

He started talking about the time Hillary claimed to have dodged sniper fire, a claim that made even my liberal friends cringe in embarrassment that Hillary had said it. Then he mentioned the staged campaign insults about Hillary going back to the kitchen to make cookies.

He didn't have to say he thought it was staged for me to realize that this was just another staged Clinton incident. My stomach felt heavy as I realized I was siding with Rush Limbaugh against Hillary Clinton, but her years of staged crisis moments had finally caught up with me. I'd finally had enough, and Rush has been the one whose words put that last straw on the camel's back.

Janet Rebels Against her Ex-Husband and Never Looks Back

Janet from New Mexico

"Dittos Rush" was a phrase I hated hearing on the radio. I always thought it meant I was about to hear some right wing jerk say things that were just going to make me angry. I usually changed the station when I heard it.

Back in January 2013 I was skimming through the radio. I was heading home from my ex-husband's sentencing hearing. He'd been molesting our son during court ordered "unsupervised visitation" and I was angry. I was hateful. I wanted to do things that I knew would make him angry.

My son, I'm never going to call him **our** son because that monster lost that right, and the courts agreed, **my** son was spending the night with my parents. I was alone in the car, and I heard "Dittos Rush" while the radio was in scan mode.

My ex husband HATED Rush Limbaugh. I HAD to listen.

I got married young and I'd never really heard of

Rush Limbaugh before I got married. I grew up in a liberal family in a liberal home, so I only kinda sorta knew the name by reputation, and it was a nasty reputation. "He hates folks like your Mom" was something my Dad said. Well, My Dad had liked my husband, and now everyone who'd agreed with that monster was suspect in my book. Rush was talking about "gay rights" and how they could lead to pedophiles getting their away, and beastiality and necrophilia and there were callers saying pretty much the same thing. They were giving examples, hypothetical ones to them but very real to me. Everything but the necrophilia reminded me of my ex husband and the things he'd done. I wouldn't put THAT past him. I suspect he'd never gone in for that just because he'd never had the chance, or if he had he'd never been caught.

I listened, for the first time I really LISTENED to a conservative. Instead of screaming "You're evil!" like I'd been taught and changing the station I payed attention and thought about what Rush Limbaugh was saying. As I listened I realized he was making a lot of sense. I ended up pulling over to give the radio my full attention. He talked about welfare leeches, and I remembered by sister-in-law with her four kids, and how the whole family was on welfare and how she was planning a fifth kid to get more money. They didn't want another kid, just more money, and they were bringing a child into the world to make that happen. All my life I'd been taught to "understand" women like my sister-in-law, but here was Rush telling me it was OK to be angry at her, OK to be frustrated, OK to not want her to keep living off my taxes. All those years of feeling guilty about being angry at her seemed wasted. Rush showed me it was OK to be angry at someone who was living off the taxpayers, no matter HOW much I loved her kids, loved my brother or even loved her.

Nearly two hours had passed by the time Rush's show ended. A LOT had been talked about and I had a LOT to think about. I drove home, and decided when I got there instead of getting drunk and calling my girlfriends to complain about my now jailed ex-husband, I'd check out Rush Limbaugh's website. He'd made a lot of sense, and so had most his callers. The most important thing was I was never going to listen to anyone tell me about gay rights again. Now I knew where that kind of talk really lead. My son was in for a lot of therapy because of "gay rights" and what my husband did to him, and I wasn't going to be silent when anyone else tried to tell me how one didn't lead to the other.

Personal Responsibility

Mark from Michigan

Back during the Clinton administration, my professional and personal life was in shambles. I'd just been fired from my fourth job in five years and my freelance design business didn't have a single client. I complained to everyone I knew about all the people whose mistakes or hostility had wronged me. I blamed women I'd worked with, accusing them of conspiring against me to get me fired. I blamed difficult customers of my design business. I blamed a printer who has messed up a poster order.

Everyone was at fault but me.

My Father had given me a battered copy of one of Rush Limbaugh's books. I read it, expecting it to help me find ways to blame liberals as well. What I found was Rush's account of how he lost his first dream job.

Like most red blooded American boys, Rush had grown up loving baseball. As an adult, he got a job as the Kansas City Royals promotions director. One of the promotions he ran was a contest to throw out the first pitch at a game. Everything went great. He boosted ticket sales with the promotion, raised some money for charity and was looking great to his bosses. Then came the day when the first winner was to throw out the first pitch of a game. It was the high point of Rush's employment with the Royals.

Then disaster struck.

He's forgotten to bring a baseball with him to the mound.

Realizing if he went to the dugout, every baseball would be hidden, Rush asked for someone to throw him a baseball. A deluge of gloves, bats, baseballs and every other piece of equipment the players could get their hands on were thrown in a tsunami of athletic gear. Rush, the contest winner and the team officials had to run to avoid getting hit.

It ended up being Rush Limbaugh's last day with the Kansas City Royals.

After reading that account I was expecting Rush to go into a tirade about irresponsible and immature players, talk about the culture of irresponsibility in professional baseball or do SOMETHING to criticise the men who got Rush fired from his dream job that day. Rush's response was the last thing I'd expected.

Rush said it was HIS fault he lost his job that day.

HE hadn't taken into account the typical behavior of the people he worked with. HE had forgotten to bring a baseball to the mound. HE accepted responsibility for HIS actions that resulted in hundreds of pounds of sports gear being strewn on the field.

I had to put the book down. It was three days before I picked it up again to reread the section.

After rereading it, I sat down and wrote out all the things that had happened at the jobs I'd lost. I thought about what I could have done differently to take into account the shortcomings of my coworkers and clients. Instead of expecting people to act as maturely as I did, I wondered what I, as the more mature one, could have done differently to work around their immaturity.

The freelance clients I'd lost were easy to work through. I should have been more patient with them and I should have taken more time to educate them on the printing and design technology needed to do what they wanted.

The fellow employees who'd "cost" me my past jobs were acting out of fear. I was a genuine threat to their jobs, and instead of ranting about how offended I was at the accusations they made up to get me fired, I should have calmly questioned the accuracy of their lies. I should have asked for evidence. Instead of getting angry with dishonest people being dishonest, I should have forced them to produce the evidence of their accusations, instead of relying on my reputation.

I wasn't unemployed for much longer. Once I accepted responsibility for how I could have changed things in the past, my failures were no longer a black mark on my resume, but a shining example of how I had LEARNED from my past. Companies always like people who can learn.

The freelance business took longer to rebuild. That was slow going, until I personally went to all the print shops I'd yelled at and apologized in person. Saying "I treated you unfairly and yelled at you for things that weren't your fault," left an impression, and it was a good one. It took some work to get some of them to hear me out, but in the end they were all pleased. Once they realized I was sincere and not just trying to get on their good sides, a few of them even started recommending my design services to their regular customers.

Thank you Rush Limbaugh, for teaching me to take responsibility for my own lot in life, and not wallow in regret and blame.

Rush Limbaugh Saved my Marriage

Eustice from Minnesota

I hated my husband because of his job. I've always been a bigger woman and my husband took a job at an ad agency during the Obama recession. He got really good at it. He started as a copyeditor and before long he was pitching whole ad campaigns.

Around the time he got the new job I started working on improving my self esteem. I'd always felt I was too fat and too ugly, and when my husband and I got married I was thrilled that a man loved me. During the recession my friends and I started talking a lot about consumerism, and how advertising made us feel ashamed of our bodies to sell us things, and how maybe the economy had crashed because women had started waking up to marketing and were standing up for ourselves. There was a lot of Earth Goddess and Fat Acceptance talk in the group.

When my husband started working for the marketing firm it caused a lot of friction with my friends. I was "sleeping with the enemy" and "betraying the sisterhood by supporting a shame-seller." I defended him at first, but when he got a contract to do a local campaign for a beauty spa I just couldn't handle it anymore. I told him he had to leave the job or I'd leave him. He told me it was the best work he could find and it was his best chance to support me and the kids. We argued for weeks about it. The angrier I got the more I got involved with liberal causes. I even helped run a fundraiser for a local Planned Parenthood clinic.

After two months of arguing we stopped talking completely. We weren't even sharing the same bed, he started sleeping on a cot in the basement. We still lived together, and still raised our kids together but we were roommates not husband and wife. That's when I got involved with the "Flush Rush"[1] campaign. My job was to listen to the Rush Limbaugh show while my husband was at work and write to anyone who advertised on the show to tell them how horrible I thought they were for supporting Rush. It was during one of my turns to listen to the Rush Limbaugh show that a caller brought up advertising. It caught my attention. That was my BIG issue and I knew my marriage was crumbling because my husband and I had disagreed about his job.

---

[1] WND MEDIA
http://www.wnd.com/2013/07/rush-flushed-broadcast-giant-dropping-limbaugh-hannity/
LIMBAUGH RESPONDS TO 'STATIONS DUMPING HIM'
Talk-radio king wants to spill beans on radio-industry shakeup
Published: 07/29/2013

The caller was talking about CNN not being able to change who it targeted with advertising. I was getting annoyed because, as liberal as I'd gotten on social issues, I still hated what Obama had been doing to the economy. I found I was kinda agreeing with the caller. After some back and forth Rush started talking about why people hated advertising.

http://www.rushlimbaugh.com/daily/2014/01/23/advertising_reflects_the_state_of_the_culture

> Oh, I see. Well, perhaps, although the advertiser community as a whole has not given up on the financial health of the 25-54 demographic. I mean, if you want to see it in action, if you want to see advertising in action, if you want to learn everything about advertising you can, just watch the Super Bowl and just watch the commercials in the Super Bowl, and you will see. I've often said, 'cause I know it to be true, and I believe it to be true, really competent advertisers have a better handle on the pulse of the culture than anybody else. It's their job. They have one job: Separate people from their money willingly. Their job is to convince John Q. Public to give up his money for whatever they convince John Q. Public he wants. In fact, socialists decry this and communists.

John Kenneth Galbraith, who I must say was one of Mr. Buckley's closest friends, big-time leftist economist, hated consumerism, hated advertising, because he looked at it as a total -- what's the word? -- it was an insult to him. He thought it was dehumanizing. He thought the whole idea of convincing people that they needed or wanted things that they didn't need or want, was an abomination. As far as he was concerned, it was exactly what's wrong with capitalism. His theory was that capitalism couldn't survive unless you made average people want things they didn't have, and he didn't think that was healthy.

Now, that's sophistry, as far as I'm concerned. That's absolutely silly, because he was denying that people have aspirations. He was offended that people wanted to improve their standard of living. He was offended that of people wanted to acquire new things as part of their pursuit of happiness. He thought the acquisition of material things -- and he's not the only one, by the way. Every communist, socialist economist in the world thinks this, that the artificial way of selling a product, and selling a product is artificial, by definition, he thinks there shouldn't be any advertising and whatever you want should be there because you want it, not because somebody has invented it to try to sell it to you.

I kid you not. I mean, he wrote books about this, this Galbraith, John Kenneth Galbraith did. He was known as John Kenneth Galbraith to the media. He was known as Ken to his friends. Advertising and consumerism, I mean, it was like showing Dracula the cross. You shouldn't want anything other than the basics -- and if you did, it was because some advertiser came along and showed it to you.

That was artificial, and it was mean, because it was showing a lot of people things they couldn't have. I mean, the way that would manifest itself is if Lamborghini advertised, that would be horrible, that would be mean, because 999 people out of a thousand would never be able to afford one. "So to show them what they can't have, that's mean, and that's what capitalism is! It's mean, and it breeds resentment and jealousy."

So he didn't like advertising at all. He didn't like consumerism, and he's not the only one. He was just the most eloquent at expressing it. On the other hand, I've always believed that if a company hires an agency to sell its product -- to market and sell its product -- that agency has to know the culture. That agency has to know cool, it has to know hip, and it has to be able to predict it, and it has to be able to personify it.

It has to be able to hire people who are it, or who recognize it, who can write it, who can produce it in TV commercials. There's all kinds of different advertising. There's cost per thousand, there's results oriented, there's impressions, any number of ways of going about it. Television advertising in the Super Bowl is a combination of cost per thousand reaching eyeballs, but also results oriented and branding.

If you watch the advertising -- actually, in anything, in any prime time show. For example, prime time, you watch any show that's targeting the 25-54 demographic, and you will learn what those people think is cool, hip, and where our culture is. So if you watch the Super Bowl and really take time to watch the commercials and study 'em rather than be entertained by 'em, you will find out you'll have a pretty good bead on where the country is culturally.

I've always believed this.

I've always believed that good advertising is a great window on where we are. Again, the reason: Even though it's established that people older than 55 have all the money, they also have everything they want, or most of it, and they've already established their brand loyalty. It would simply cost too much to get them to change their minds. That's why you start studying this and you'll see that most commercials are done and aimed at people in their teens and twenties.

I turned off the radio when he finished. I started thinking about Ferraris and Beauty Queens. I'd never own a Ferrari and I'd never be a beauty queen, but I was angry at people for advertising things I'd never have just because they were selling them.

I thought about my diabetic mother, and how before she died she'd always yell at the television when the Dunkin Donuts man said it was "Time to make the donuts." I liked donuts, and I thought the commercials were funny. My mother hated them because they were selling something she could never have. Was my crusade against diet pills and makeup advertising really that different than my mother's hate for donut advertising? I hated my husband just because he was selling things I'd never have. I was mad at my husband for selling people things that weren't right for me, but was it really OK for me to keep other people from hearing about these products just because I couldn't use them?

My husband sold things that made the beautiful people look even better, but even after two months of sleeping in the basement, he still hadn't cheated on me and still hadn't started talking about divorce. He still loved me just the way I was even though he sold things I could never use without looking like a fool.

I cried until it was time to pick the kids up from school. After I fed them and helped them with their homework I cried until I sent them to bed and then I cried until my husband came home. When he saw me he didn't bring up the months of arguments, he just asked me what was wrong.

He hasn't slept on the cot in the basement since, and we don't argue about his job anymore. I have some new friends though. Most of them are just as fat as I am, but they don't lecture me on needing to stomp out advertising that sells beauty products or diet pills. Ads for products we'll never use are just a good time to get a fresh glass of tea.

Knowing the Good Guys from the Bad Guys

Billy from California

It's hard, ya know? You listen to the Radio, watch TV and read the Internet and everyone has their own thing to say, their own side to pick. I'd bet if you went looking you could find someone pushing every possible side of an issue, sort of a quantum theory of social politics. Some egghead, ivory tower physics types think every possible reality exists, out there, somewhere. I think some of them just say that cuz they hope there's a universe out there where they're popular. But they kinda have a point about opinions, everyone has one, and with seven billion of us on Earth, just about every opinion you CAN have is rattling around on someone's head. There are even folks who think global warming is REAL if you can believe that, not just liberals pushing it as an excuse to control us, but honest to God true believers in that nonsense.

Anyway, not long ago, I was kinda on the fence about a lot of things. I kinda saw both sides of the whole Israel / Palestine thing, I thought all the Muslim extremists had been pushed there by good intentioned Westerners who'd screwed up, you now, the whole bleeding heart "We can all get along if we try to understand each other" thing. I thought I was a big, smart guy because I listened to every side I could before I formed my own opinion. "Oh, you only get your news from ONE source? Well, that's so VERY 1950's." This meant I was as likely to check out Rush Limbaugh as NPR.

ISIS was in the news, this whole new terrorist group we'd never heard of who was tearing up the Middle East. They were beheading children and putting their heads on spikes because they were Christian or the wrong kind of Muslim. There wasn't ANYONE defending them, because they were, finally, an enemy so evil nobody COULD side with them. Even Iran, a country we kinda need to nuke into the stone age, was sending troops to fight ISIS.

That's when I was listening to Rush Limbaugh. He started off talking about some has-been reporter who used to be a big deal, and how this wrinkled reporter wanted to hold off on attacking ISIS and didn't want to hear from anybody unless they had a kid in the military. It was wearing kinda thin to me, and I was fixin to change the station when Rush changed the topic a bit. He started talking about how Obama has been siding with ISIS[2], how he'd

---

[2] Obama Almost Allied with ISIS Against Assad in Syria
Aug 25, 2014
https://www.rushlimbaugh.com/daily/2014/08/25/obama_almos
t_allied_with_isis_against_assad_in_syria/

been getting ready to bomb an ISIS enemy back into the stone age because ISIS was kinda good at making it look like the democratically elected Syrian president was gassing his own people.

I was blown away. Syria was our ally in the war on terror. They'd done a lot of the interrogations that Democrat backed hand-tying laws kept us from doing ourselves. Now here was Obama getting ready to bomb our ally because terrorists were trying to frame them.

That's when I realized that by listening to so many different people, I was getting confused. I was letting this mish-mash of ideas all ferment into something I thought was "unbiased truth" when all I really got was confused. Obama almost bombed our ally in the War on Terror because he listened to a bunch of people who weren't trustworthy. He didn't filter out the folks he couldn't trust, he gave everyone a chance to talk, and he almost handed the country of Syria to ISIS because of it.

I'm more careful with who I pay attention to now. I don't give the time of day to folks I know I can't trust. That's a lesson Rush Limbaugh taught me.

The Thug and the Cop

Francois, Missouri

I was angry at a cop I'd never met. I hated him. I wanted to see him jailed for the rest of his life for murder. When I heard the person he'd shot was fleeing a violent robbery, I didn't believe it, until the dead guy's own lawyer confirmed it was true. When I heard the officer who'd fired the gun had half his face crushed, an eye possibly blinded, by the dead man before he was shot, I dismissed it because it came from a "biased conservative source." Even the autopsy, consistent with a man being shot while attacking, didn't convince me. The news that he was high on pot gave me pause, but then I thought, "Who gets violent on pot?"

But it all added up. Every little piece of information made me less and less comfortable with the media's version of events. Then a friend sent me a quote from Rush Limbaugh.

> You know, one of the problems here, Bill, is that most people, there are a lot of exceptions, but most people respect the cops. Most people, when they're pulled over, do everything the cop tells 'em to do. So most people do not encounter an abusive cop or a cop that plants evidence.

That's a very rare occurrence. Sometimes cops get it wrong on moving traffic violations, this kind of thing. But most people, their own personal experience is one of obeying the cops.

And I think most people who are not politically active and don't think of politics when they hear a story like this, think that everybody else probably treats cops with respect, too. And therefore, when they hear the media, who they also believe, sadly say that we had a runaway cop here who shot an innocent kid, they probably think the kid was cooperating with the cop just like they do. I think it's a factor.

But there's a larger point here. And I get your point, your action fits reaction, but there's a larger point here. And it is this: We have an entire media apparatus that is making it abundantly clear that they are more than willing to create a total lie out of a circumstance like this, or they're more than willing to go along with one. They're more than willing to help establish that something happened that didn't happen. Now, why? And there is where politics enters the equation. - Rush Limbaugh, August, 2014[3]

---

[3] Democrats and the Their Media Mythmakers Hijacked

It was like he gave voice to all these little doubts that had been building up about the story. Why were we angry about what the cop did? Why was all this anger being spread on the airwaves over a case that was still being investigated? Then I saw the news about the voter drive being held at the site where the guy was shot. That's when everything clicked for me. I remembered Acorn getting Obama elected through voter fraud. I thought about how every opinion poll said Democrats should be extinct, but they still managed to get elected in areas with the highest reports of voter fraud.

I did some more reading. The people describing the dead man as a thug and a criminal had sources and evidence. The people calling him a "good kid" had all the denial of a mother whose son was just caught shooting up a preschool. Lots of emotion and no facts.

When I finished weeding out the good sources from the bad, I didn't see an innocent man who was gunned down for being black in front of a white cop. I saw a career criminal on drugs who'd committed a violent robbery, tried to kill a police officer with his bare hands and nearly managed it before the officer emptied his clip into his attacker. The

the Brown Family Tragedy for the November Election
Aug 26, 2014 https://www.rushlimbaugh.com

autopsy even proved the guy didn't go down until the sixth shot.

I'll never again take the news at face value. The bias and agenda of the REPORTER is as big a part of the story as the story itself.

 **Hannah Cøwan**
@HannahBCowan

Lets take a moment to honor the fact that my very hippy sister voted republican for the first time yesterday 🐵 #TheresHopeAfterAll

RETWEET LIKES
1   19

8:11 AM - 5 Nov 2014

↩ 2   ♻ 1   ♥ 19   •••

Obamacare Revelation

Terrance from Ohio

I'm retired, and I've been a liberal most my life. I was excited about Obamacare because it reminded me of the liberal government paid health care available in most of Europe. I teased my conservative friends about Romney, pointing out that Obamacare was pretty much the same thing Romney signed into law when he was governor of Massachusetts, the bluest state in the nation.

"And Romney says it's too expensive to do at the Federal level," was the typical response. "He would know."

I should have remembered an incident during the Vietnam war. I was doing factory work while waiting to be drafted. One day a prize chump came up and drove the forklift into some shelving, sending the whole unit, and about $25,000 worth of stock, smashing to the ground. That's a lot of money now, but it was a lot MORE back then. At the review the next day he expected to be fired, but the boss told him he'd "just invested 25 grand in your education, and I expect to get my money back." The idiot kept his job because the boss expected him to learn from his mistakes. Mitt Romney was that joker, the idiot who wasted a lot of money. Romney learned his mistake by signing a bad bill into law, and he didn't want to repeat it.

I didn't realize what a big mistake Romney didn't want to repeat until I went to see my cardiologist in the late Summer of 2004. Instead of the short lines and short wait I was used to, I had to stand in line behind several people. Instead of one secretary processing everyone within minutes of walking in the door, there were three of them, and one of them took over half an hour to check in one patient. I was wondering what was going on when the woman in front of me, a good 10 years my senior, started complaining about Obama.

"Damn Obamacare," She said. "Now we got all these people gumming up the works who would stay home waiting to ACTUALLY get sick but now because they got all those Obamacare plans they come and go like it's nothing, eating up all the money in the system and wasting the time of every doctor in the place." I thought about what she'd said while I waited. The new secretary was STILL trying to check in a new patient, and I didn't recognize her. She was new. She'd been hired to deal with all the new Obamacare patients and she hadn't been trained up yet. The woman in line ahead of me went on, and I told her I though she made some good points.

That's when the guy in front of both of us decided

to join the conversation. He had to be 30 at most, and he looked well fed and robust, not the sickly look you get with men who've had cardiac problems since childhood. "I have Obamacare," he said, drawing out the "I" like we might miss it if he didn't. "And the hospital's not full because of Obamacare. Just look at the statistics. It's full because OLD people like YOU TWO just WON'T DIE!"

"Who do you work for son?" I asked.

"I'm self employed!" he said proudly, puffing out his chest. I wondered how he could do that if he was REALLY sick enough to need a cardiologist at his age.

"What do you make?" I asked.

He deflated like a balloon. I figured that meant "Not much."

"It's the taxes from 'old people' like me what pay for your medical care son," I said. "I KNOW you ain't paying in enough to pay for this visit, so don't sass me child."

He turned around and faced back towards the front of the line. None of us said anything for the rest of our time in line. When he checked in he slunk off to sit down, avoiding eye contact with both of us.

"This is what I voted for," I thought. This is what my friends kept telling me Rush Limbaugh was warning us about. This is why he'd said if Obama was elected he'd fly overseas for his medical care. All my happy, feel-good ideas about helping the poor and all I did was infect the health care system with parasites. The waiting room was nearly full, and most of the people there were folks I didn't recognize, folks who I bet didn't have nothing wrong with them a little exercise wouldn't cure.

And here I was, wasting my time, waiting for people to see my doctor on my tax dime for ills that they'd have been fine dealing with on their own a home without Obamacare.

I'm never voting Democrat again.

UN Smears Against a Christian Soldier

Joe from Montana

I hadn't listened to Rush Limbaugh in a few years. Disgusted with politics, I was making an effort to avoid the topic. I'd even given up on the Republican party. As happens when you bury your head far enough in the sand, I started drifting towards the left, swayed by the tear-jerker stories people told. One day, my liberal friends, who at the time made up the majority of the people I knew on Facebook, were posting article after article about Rush Limbaugh. They were furious that he had said something positive about something called the LRA,[4] a group none of us had ever heard of before Rush mentioned them.

While I'd been a dedicated Dittohead a few years before, I'd spent enough time among liberals to have the typical "Rush is a villain" knee-jerk reaction. I started reading the articles people had posted, but they were more hyperbole than hard facts, so I sought out Rush's actual words.

---

[4] Christian Science Monitor "Why did Rush Limbaugh defend Joseph Kony and Lord's Resistance Army By Peter Grier, MARCH 9, 2012

*RUSH: President Obama has deployed
troops to another war, in Africa, ladies and
gentlemen. Jacob Tapper, ABC News, is
reporting that Obama has sent 100 US
troops to Uganda to help combat Lord's
Resistance Army. Tapper reporting today:
"Two days ago President Obama authorized
the deployment to Uganda of approximately
100 combat-equipped U.S. forces to help
regional forces 'remove from the battlefield'
-- meaning capture or kill -- Lord's
Resistance Army leader Joseph Kony and
senior leaders of the LRA." I wonder how
the Wall Street crowd is gonna react when
they find out that Obama has sent troops to
another war? "Mr. Limbaugh, it's just 100
peacekeepers." Yep, yep, yep, that's how
Libya started, and, by the way, there's no
end in sight for Libya.*

*"The forces will deploy beginning with a
small group and grow over the next month
to 100. They will ultimately go to Uganda,
South Sudan, the Central African Republic,
and the Democratic Republic of the Congo."
A hundred people are gonna go to all those
places? "The president made this
announcement in a letter to House Speaker*

John Boehner, R-Ohio, Friday afternoon, saying that 'deploying these U.S. Armed Forces furthers U.S. national security interests and foreign policy and will be a significant contribution toward counter-LRA efforts in central Africa.'" LRA is Lord's Resistance Army. And it doesn't mean God's resistance army. Lord is some Lord, some guy. A "Defense Department official tells ABC's Luis Martinez at the Pentagon that the U.S. troops will be in Africa 'for a few months in an advisory role.'" One hundred troops in an advisory role.

So nothing to worry about here, folks, only gonna be for a few months. Now, up until today, most Americans have never heard of the combat Lord's Resistance Army. And here we are at war with them. Have you ever heard of Lord's Resistance Army, Dawn? How about you, Brian? Snerdley, have you? You never heard of Lord's Resistance Army? Well, proves my contention, most Americans have never heard of it, and here we are at war with them. Lord's Resistance Army are Christians. It means God. I was only kidding. Lord's Resistance Army are Christians. They are fighting the Muslims in Sudan. And Obama has sent troops, United States troops to remove them from the battlefield, which means kill them. That's what the lingo means, "to help regional forces remove from the battlefield," meaning capture or kill.

So that's a new war, a hundred troops to wipe out Christians in Sudan, Uganda, and -- (interruption) no, I'm not kidding. Jacob Tapper just reported it. Now, are we gonna help the Egyptians wipe out the Christians? Wouldn't you say that we are? I mean the Coptic Christians are being wiped out, but it wasn't just Obama that supported that. The conservative intelligentsia thought it was an outbreak of democracy. Now they've done a 180 on that, but they forgot that they supported it in the first place. Now they're criticizing it.

Lord's Resistance Army objectives. I have them here. "To remove dictatorship and stop the oppression of our people." Now, again Lord's Resistance Army is who Obama sent troops to help nations wipe out. The objectives of the Lord's Resistance Army, what they're trying to accomplish with their military action in these countries is the following: "To remove dictatorship and stop the oppression of our people; to fight for the immediate restoration of the competitive multiparty democracy in Uganda; to see an end to gross violation of human rights and dignity of Ugandans; to ensure the restoration of peace and security in Uganda, to ensure unity, sovereignty, and economic prosperity beneficial to all Ugandans, and to bring to an end the repressive policy of deliberate marginalization of groups of people who may not agree with the LRA ideology." Those are the objectives of the group that we are fighting, or who are being fought and we are joining in the effort to remove them from the battlefield.

The government of Uganda claims that Lord's Resistance Army only has 500 or a thousand soldiers in total. So what's the threat? If that's the maximum size of their army, what's the threat? A thousand soldiers? Now, 1100 soldiers because we have sent a hundred. I'm not making this up. This is Jacob Tapper. ABC News had reported that Obama got a letter off to John Boehner a couple days ago announcing this. It's just for a few months until the Lord's Resistance Army is eradicated. That's all. Just a few months. Not much of a threat.

The liberal media was up in arms. They described Koney as genocidal lunatic, a madman who slaughtered innocent people, a man who forced the children of his murder victims into life as child soldiers. If even a fraction of the things they said about him were true, then Rush was a fool to side with Kony. I decided that learning the truth was more important than politics, so I started digging.

The logical starting place was Kony's Wikipedia page.

http://en.wikipedia.org/wiki/Joseph_Kony

The secret to using Wikipedia is to ignore the article itself and pay attention to the references that support the claims in the article. For example, most climate change articles are stuffed to the gills with citations from liberal think tanks and university "research" departments. The Joseph Kony article was full of a lot of serious accusations all backed up by citations, but the citations were where the real meat was. **Almost all the sources were UN funded groups.** Most of Joseph Kony's bad press came from the UN and organizations funded by it. The few references I found that weren't directly funded by the UN were just repeating claims made by U.N. funded groups.

When I stripped away the U.N. funded "information" I was left with very little:

Joseph Kony and his group claim to be Christian.

Joseph Kony and his group say they support Democracy

Joseph Kony and his group are fighting a guerilla war against a Communist government.

That's it. That's ALL we really know about Joseph Kony that doesn't come from the UN.

By the time I was wrapping up my research I'd learned that the director of the Kony2012 video making the rounds was probably gay.[5]

I was left with a simple choice. Who was I going to believe, Rush Limbaugh, or the U.N., who I knew was out to oppress and marginalize my fellow Christians?

I chose to side with Rush.

Update
Editor's note. Six months after this narrative was originally submitted, the following update was received from the original author. It has been added to this book in the second edition to further illustrate that Rush Was Right.

---

[5] Kony 2012 founder tells Oprah he's not gay... 'just theatrical' (claims he didn't recover from his naked, ranting breakdown for TWO WEEKS)
PUBLISHED: 8 October 2012 dailymail.co.uk

I lost a few liberal "friends" after I started talking about what we really knew about Kony when you stripped away the UN propaganda. That was OK. Most my friends realized I was right when Jason Russell, the activist who kicked it all off with a slickly produced video for "Invisible Children," was arrested for running around naked, in public, committing obscene acts in front of children. While a lot of the Hollywood elite will side with a sex offender if they like his movies, most rank and file Democrats are still sane enough to not side with a sex offender. Russell's perversion gave me proof of that. When news circulated that Kony was probably dead [6] anyway, it seemed to be the last nail in the coffin's lid.

Just when I thought there was no more to tell, I learned Russell was the founder of Invisible Children, the charity that produced the video. It raked in $20 MILLION from gullible Liberals [7] after the video came out. The charity was making money as fast as they could print "Kony 2012" shirts and their internet traffic was being paid for by YouTube; despite this they STILL managed to spend over $6 Million in expenses. Russell's financial motive in towing the U..N. line on Kony was clear. Even the

---

[6] Is it possible Joseph Kony is dead?
2012-04-25 news24.com

[7] Remember Kony 2012? Well, it's 2013. What happened?
JANUARY 11, 2013 news.com.au

Ugandans, whose nation was supposedly being torn apart by Kony, criticized the video[8] as described by Moni Basu for CNN.

> *But with the popularity of the video and kudos to the filmmakers for raising awareness of an African tragedy came a flurry of questions about Invisible Children's intentions, its transparency and whether the social media frenzy was too little, too late.*
>
> *… "If people cared 15 years ago, then thousands of lives would have been saved and thousands of children would have stayed at home and not been kidnapped."*
>
> *But the media attention on Kony may actually hamper efforts to catch Kony, said Peter Pham of the Atlantic Council.*
>
> *"All I can say is, it couldn't have happened at a more unhelpful moment when you look at it strategically and operationally," said Pham, a civilian adviser to the military command that sent the U.S. troops.*
>
> ***The film comes after a regional -- and covert -- military operation has been***

---

[8] As criticism surfaces, 'KONY 2012' gains momentum faster than Susan Boyle
By Moni Basu, CNN.com Tue March 13, 2012

under way for several months. The attention could prompt Kony[or his surviving lieutenants] to go on the move again and seriously set back African and U.S. efforts to catch Kony once and for all. -Moni Basu, CNN

Even the Ugandan government, which Russell's "charity" claimed to support, had harsh words for Russell's propaganda video.

[The Ugandan Government] *said Invisible Children and other advocacy groups "have* **manipulated facts for strategic purposes,** *exaggerating the scale of LRA abductions and murders and emphasizing the LRA's use of innocent children as soldiers."*

"They rarely refer to the Ugandan atrocities or those of Sudan's People's Liberation Army, such as attacks against civilians or looting of civilian homes and businesses, or the complicated regional politics fueling the conflict."

Invisible Children addressed the criticisms on its website, [admitting] it simplified a complex crisis. -Moni Basu, CNN

That's right. The "charity" that made the video

Ugandans, whose nation was supposedly being torn apart by Kony, criticized the video[8] as described by Moni Basu for CNN.

> But with the popularity of the video and kudos to the filmmakers for raising awareness of an African tragedy came a flurry of questions about Invisible Children's intentions, its transparency and whether the social media frenzy was too little, too late.
>
> … "If people cared 15 years ago, then thousands of lives would have been saved and thousands of children would have stayed at home and not been kidnapped."
>
> But the media attention on Kony may actually hamper efforts to catch Kony, said Peter Pham of the Atlantic Council.
>
> "All I can say is, it couldn't have happened at a more unhelpful moment when you look at it strategically and operationally," said Pham, a civilian adviser to the military command that sent the U.S. troops.
>
> **The film comes after a regional -- and covert -- military operation has been**

[8] As criticism surfaces, 'KONY 2012' gains momentum faster than Susan Boyle
By Moni Basu, CNN.com Tue March 13, 2012

under way for several months. The attention could prompt Kony[or his surviving lieutenants] to go on the move again and seriously set back African and U.S. efforts to catch Kony once and for all. -Moni Basu, CNN

Even the Ugandan government, which Russell's "charity" claimed to support, had harsh words for Russell's propaganda video.

> [The Ugandan Government] *said Invisible Children and other advocacy groups "have **manipulated facts for strategic purposes**, exaggerating the scale of LRA abductions and murders and emphasizing the LRA's use of innocent children as soldiers."*
>
> *"They rarely refer to the Ugandan atrocities or those of Sudan's People's Liberation Army, such as attacks against civilians or looting of civilian homes and businesses, or the complicated regional politics fueling the conflict."*
>
> ***Invisible Children addressed the criticisms on its website, [admitting] it simplified a complex crisis.*** -Moni Basu, CNN

That's right. The "charity" that made the video

ADMITTED they were "simplifying" things.

Then there's the racism in Russell's approach.

> *Richard Downie, a fellow and deputy director of the Africa Program at the Center for Strategic and International Studies, took issue with an approach he said was focused on the white Westerner's ability to parachute in and resolve a problem that Africans are unable to deal with themselves.*
>
> *"I think by portraying Westerners as the only people who can crack this problem of Joseph Kony -- it's simplistic, it's naive, and it's a little bit condescending as well," he said.* -Moni Basu, CNN

Typical U.S. Liberal, thinking it's their job to go in and save everyone, because the liberal professors in their Ivory Tower HAVE to know better than the folks who have boots on the ground, right?

Even the U.N. has softened its stance on Kony, admitting that Atrocities by Both Sides in the South Sudan War[9] mean at least one of Kony's battlegrounds isn't a war where the good guys are

---

[9] U.N. Report Documents Atrocities by Both Sides in South Sudan War
By ISMA'IL KUSHKUSH and SOMINI SENGUPTAMAY 8, 2014 nytimes.com

fighting the bad guys, but a bunch of bad guys fighting for control of land that's been soaked in blood for generations. Kony's real role in the Sudan conflict is shrouded in U.N. propaganda, but the Sudanese government he's fighting has to be pretty bad for even the U.N. to admit Kony may not be the villain in that theater.

The harder you look, the clearer, and more disturbing the picture becomes. Instead of a crusader trying to raise awareness of a mass murdering, genocidal lunatic, we see a money-grabbing sex offender making a slick video about an obscure U.N. scapegoat to rake in 20 million dollars.

Don't fall for the liberal propaganda. Obama sent US troops into danger, committing us to a brand new quagmire, all because a sex offender wanted to make some money. Rush was Right. Obama was Wrong.

Flip The Senate

I didn't believe any of the polls about a Republican takeover of the Senate in the 2014 mid-term elections. I was sure it was propaganda, or we'd be able to pull out a last minute victory like we did when Obama was running against McCain for President. When the predicted flip happened, I was shocked. I was despondent. I was sure there'd been some mistake. I had friends who tried to blame new Voter ID laws, but those laws hadn't even gone into effect yet. I had no idea what to think until my Mother emailed me a link to Rush Limbaugh's website. It was a transcript from his show.

Caller's Great Point: If Voters Wanted Congress to Work with Obama, They Would've Elected Democrats[10]

There really wasn't much more to say. If I was going to continue being proud of living in a democracy, I had to accept the fact that my fellow Americans had rejected Obama and his policies.

The more I thought about it the more sense the results made. Obama had failed to provide the

---

[10] Caller's Great Point: If Voters Wanted Congress to Work with Obama, They Would've Elected Democrats Nov 6, 2014 rushlimbaugh.com

"Hope and Change" he'd promised. The economic crash caused by his election had dragged on for years, he bungled our efforts to leave Iraq, he created a new terrorist group that formed a whole new country inside the borders of other Muslim nations. He was a failure, and as much as I wanted to be a Democrat, I had to turn my back on him.

I still want a Democrat to win in 2016, but now I understand that I need to think more about the person running and less about if he has the magical "(D)" after his name in news reports. This time, I'm voting for the best man running, not the best Democrat running. If that means I vote Republican, so be it.

Giving up on Obama

Ray from New York

Fip the Senate, Flip the Senate, Flip the Senate. It's all I heard for months in 2014 and I wasn't very surprised when it went and happened. The Democrats needed the youth vote to get elected and unless a President was running the youth just don't care enough to bother voting. I was sure it was the apathy of the young and nothing else that turned the senate red to match the house. I was angry.

I'm a big Colbert fan. I watch him regularly. I've been a fan since he started off as a parody of that stupid stuffed shirt Bill O'Reilly. The more his character evolved the funnier it got. One night, not long after the elections, he was playing a clip from Rush Limbaugh.[11] Rush was talking about how the GOP hadn't been elected to govern, but to stop Obama. Colbert was trying to make a joke about the GOP not governing, but the crowd started chanting "Stop Obama, Stop Obama."

That's when it hit me. The youth vote hadn't failed because the youth didn't find midterm elections sexy, it failed because Obama had failed the

---

[11] Editor's Note: November 10, 2014 episode of *The Colbert Report*

Democratic party, and the Democrats hadn't seen anyone running worth voting for. The youth hadn't failed the Democrats, Obama had failed the Democrats and the youth.

I turned off the TV and went to bed.

Scott Robison
@CasaDeRobison

Follow

RT @iowahawkblog
Bad news: you lost your seat because you voted for Obamacare.
Worse news: now you're covered by Obamacare.

8:32 AM - 5 Nov 2014

Anonymous Confession

This was sent to the editors using a "burner" email address forwarded through the TOR Anonymizing Network. It is presented here unedited, with no grammar or spelling correction. The real author is unknown.

Peter,

I own a businesses in Philadelphia. I ignored the debate about increasing the minimum wage. I thought nobody was stupid enough to pay entry level high shcol dropouts more than our soldiers. I was wrong. I did my projections for next year and Im screwed. I cant decrease head count or I'll get nothing done. I cna't charge more because most my customers can't afford it. I know two guys already shutting up shop before the pay increase and another working on bankruptcy papers. He gon burn on until it all goes south and leave the taxpayers to clean up when he goes bankrupts paying the new minimum wage.

I got a plan. I got it from Rush. There's a few places in town where illegals hang out waiting for work. I'm gonna hire them instead of the expensive citizens. Hiking the minimum wage got me to hire illegals. I'm firing a bunch of the guys I got now. I need to make it look like the legals are doing the work and the illeglas aren't there but I can handle that.

I'm not writin to taunt. If I wanted to taunt I'd write to the popo or immigration. I'm writing to tell the folks what listen that minimum wasge is stupid and just means money goes to Mexico through illegls and not americans.

Editor's Note: This letter appears to be referring to the following clip from the November 11, 2014 episode of the Rush Limbaugh Show.

> RUSH: I hope Clarence in Philadelphia is still listening, reveling in his big victory out there. Clarence, you know what's gonna happen in all these states where the minimum wage was increased? Employers are gonna hire more and more illegal aliens off the books at lower wages. The minimum wage actually facilitates the hiring of illegals if we're gonna let 'em in the country, Clarence. Big win, huh?

I Lost my LEG for this Jerk

"Fang" from Oklahoma

Far as I know every man in my family has served in the military since they started allowing enlistment from the Oklahoma territories. My brothers and I didn't see eye to eye on a lot of things growing up, but hunting and the military always brought us together. Even when I started voting for Democrats we were still together about enlisting when we graduated from high school.

I didn't approve of the Iraq war. When I was a kid I thought we should have let Saddam have Kuwait, it wasn't any of our business. When W. said Saddam had WMDs, I didn't believe it. I still enlisted. It was my duty to my country. I didn't surprise anyone I was REALLY bitter when I lost a leg to an IED in Iraq. One aunt called it "Ironic justice." I never found out what "Justice" she thought was served because one of my sisters decked her for it and in the interest of family peace, I haven't asked her about it since.

Still, as hard as it hurt, even the other Democrats I knew had my back. The same people who joined me in condemning the war for being based on lies still thanked me for my service and called me a hero. My Grandpa served in 'Nam, and he told me it felt good to see folks call me a hero and not a Babykiller, even when they thought the war was unjust.

Then I got an email from the aunt who'd called it "Justice" I lost a leg to an IED. The subject line read "This is what you side with blue boy." "Blue Boy" was the nickname she started using for me once the whole "Red State / Blue State" thing caught on. She took my politics powerful personal, and I had half a mind to delete the email without reading it.

When I opened the email it was just a link to Rush Limbaugh's website.

http://www.rushlimbaugh.com/daily/2014/11/11/vile _salon_columnist_trashes_military_law_enforceme nt

I clicked it and started reading. Rush was talking about an article from Salon.com. The more I read, the angrier I got.

> It's from Salon.com. It ran this past Sunday. And here is the headline: "You Don't Protect My Freedom: Our Childish Insistence on Calling Soldiers Heroes Deadens Real Democracy -- It's been 70 years since we fought a war about freedom. Forced troop worship and compulsory patriotism must end.

You Don't Protect My Freedom: Our Childish Insistence on Calling Soldiers Heroes Deadens Real Democracy.

Put a man in uniform, preferably a white man, give him a gun, and Americans will worship him. It is a particularly childish trait, of a childlike culture, that insists on anointing all active military members and police officers as "heroes." The rhetorical sloppiness and intellectual shallowness of affixing such a reverent label to everyone in the military or law enforcement betrays a frightening cultural streak of nationalism, chauvinism, authoritarianism and totalitarianism, but it also makes honest and serious conversations necessary for the maintenance and enhancement of a fragile democracy nearly impossible.

I saw what life was like for people who didn't have the freedoms this jackass was asking me to stop defending. I saw what happens when there's no police, no military to really protect a man's rights. I was in a place where the "good guys" chopped the hands off petty thieves and executed rape VICTIMS as an "honor killing." That Shia vs Sunni violence you keep hearing about in the news? That's a religious war. For Christians it'd be like Baptists and Methodists being locked in a centuries old blood feud, doing their best to kill each other off. Here in the US, a Baptist will vote for a Catholic. In Iraq, the Shia voters try to ASSASSINATE the Sunni candidates, and that goes both ways.

I read the Salon article and Masciotra was the single most petty, ivory tower bastard I ever read. He lived down to every stereotype, every insult, every negative thing anyone ever said the me about voting Democrat, only he wasn't a misunderstanding or election time politics. He was real. He really WAS as vile, disgusting and delusional as the worst stereotypes my aunt had of Democrats.

After I calmed down I wrote my aunt back.

"I never met a Democrat like that in Oklahoma or in the service. That man gives everyone I've ever met a bad name."

A couple days later she wrote back.

"You've never met a real Democrat. You've only met young Republicans who let their hearts bleed all over their shirts."

Metaphors were never something she was good at, but I got what she was saying. The hard part was, I think she's right.

More to come

This Third Edition is just the beginning. Do you want your account of Rush Limbaugh showing you the light included in the next edition? Contact the editor, Peter Cornswalled at Peter.Cornswalled@gmail.com

Like the book? Leave us a five star Amazon review! The more people know, the more the word will spread about how Rush is RIGHT!

ISBN: 978-1499325249

Crime Fic
and the
Indie
Contribut

Chris Longmuir

B&J

This book is dedicated to all those indie authors and publishers who are publishing quality books for discerning readers.

CONTENTS